Courage!

COURAGE!

*Personal Experiences of Challenge and Decision
in the Lives of Great Men and Women*

*Selected by Peter Seymour
Illustrated by Robert Brickhouse*

♛ **Hallmark Editions**

"An Indestructible Radiance" from *Party of One* by Clifton Fadiman, first published in the *New Yorker* magazine, Copyright © 1955 by Clifton Fadiman, reprinted by permission of The World Publishing Company. "Why Franco Never Took Madrid" (Copyright 1937 New York Times Company and North American Newspaper Alliance; renewal Copyright © 1964 Mary Hemingway) reprinted with the permission of Charles Scribner's Sons and William Collins Sons & Co. Ltd. from *By-Line: Ernest Hemingway,* pages 271-274, edited by William White. "The Spirit of St. Louis" reprinted with the permission of Charles Scribner's Sons and John Murray Ltd. from *The Spirit of St. Louis,* pages 326-329, by Charles Lindbergh, Copyright 1953 Charles Scribner's Sons. "Keeping Ideals" from *The Works of Anne Frank,* Copyright © 1959 by Otto H. Frank, reprinted by permission of Doubleday & Company, Inc. and Vallentine, Mitchell & Co., Ltd. "He Jarred the Sagging Chins" from *Seven Came Through* by Captain Edward V. Rickenbacker, Copyright 1943 by Doubleday & Company, Inc. and reprinted with their permission. "John Glenn's Glory Ride" from *American Space Exploration* by William Roy Shelton, Copyright © 1960, 1963, 1967, 1968 by William Roy Shelton, reprinted by permission of Little, Brown & Co. and Harold Matson Co., Inc. "The Mosquito Armada" from *Memoirs of the Second World War* by Winston Churchill, Copyright 1948-1959, reprinted by permission of Houghton Mifflin Co. and The Daily Telegraph of London. "A Clarion Call Sounded" from *Heroes for Our Times* edited by Will Yolen and Kenneth Giniger, Copyright 1968, reprinted by permission of Stackpole Books. "Man Overboard" from *Kon-Tiki* by Thor Heyerdahl, Copyright 1950 by Thor Heyerdahl, published in the United States by Rand McNally & Co. and elsewhere by George Allen & Unwin Ltd. "The Last March" reprinted by permission of Dodd, Mead & Co., Inc. from *Scott's Last Expedition* by Robert F. Scott, Copyright 1913, 1941 by Dodd, Mead & Company, Inc. "The Human Spirit Is Like a Cork" from *Brave Men* by Ernie Pyle, Copyright 1943, 1944 by Scripps-Howard Newspaper Alliance and Holt, Rinehart and Winston, Inc., reprinted by permission of Holt, Rinehart and Winston, Inc. "A Logic of Courage" by Lowell Thomas, Copyright © 1947-1959 by Newspapers Magazine Corp., reprinted by permission of Simon & Schuster, Inc. "J.F.K.'s PT109" reprinted by permission of McGraw-Hill Book Co. from *PT-109* by Robert Donovan, Copyright © 1961 by Robert J. Donovan. "To the Summit!" from *High Adventure* by Edmund Hillary, Copyright 1955, reprinted by permission of Hodder & Stoughton, Ltd. "The Lady With a Lamp" reprinted by permission of McGraw-Hill Book Company from *Florence Nightingale* by Cecil Woodham-Smith, Copyright © 1951 by Cecil Woodham-Smith. "It Isn't Courage" from the book, *All But My Life,* by Stirling Moss face-to-face with Ken W. Purdy, Copyright © 1963, Stirling Moss Ltd., reprinted, permission of E. P. Dutton & Co., Inc.

Copyright © 1969 by Hallmark Cards Inc., Kansas City, Missouri. All Rights Reserved. Printed in the United States of America. Library of Congress Catalog Card Number: 77-88791. Standard Book Number: 87529-017-5.

Contents

Dauntless in What They Do: Page 7

The Courage of Conviction: Page 31

Heroism in War: Page 43

*Courage is not simply one of the virtues,
but the form of every virtue at the testing point,
which means at the point of highest reality.
A chastity or honesty or mercy which yields to danger
will be chaste or honest or merciful only on conditions.
Pilate was merciful till it became risky.*
C. S. Lewis

Dauntless In What They Do

'IT ISN'T COURAGE'

Sports-car racing, "the most dangerous and demanding sport man has been able to devise for himself" according to one expert, has had few drivers so battered and so successful as Britisher Stirling Moss. Here Moss relives past accidents and describes his unusually calm reactions to crises:

I've been truly frightened twice, or perhaps I should say, the two times I was most frightened were at Monza [Grand Prix, Italy] in 1958 and Spa [Grand Prix, Belgium] in 1960. At Monza I was doing 160 miles an hour or so in a Maserati, when the steering sheared on the banking, the wheel just came loose in my hands, it was no longer connected to anything. I had time to think about it, to try to find something to do, but there was nothing for it, I stood on the brakes, which were nothing, they were sportscar brakes, you couldn't even feel them bite at that speed, then I thought maybe I could steer it by holding the bare steering-shaft between my feet, which was silly, of course, but gives you an idea how bad the situation really was; I knew I just had to sit and wait . . . I had

It isn't courage, it's just a case of overcoming whatever it is that worries you.

to be killed. I was sure we were going over the top of the banking. I ripped steel posts out of the concrete for more than fifty yards. That car slid for a quarter of a mile, blowing its tyres, buckling the wheels, breaking itself up . . . when it stopped, and right side up, I was surprised to find myself alive, I can tell you that. I hardly believe it.

The other time was when the wheel came off in Belgium. I was doing perhaps 140 miles an hour when the car suddenly went into a very violent oversteer condition. First I thought I had hit oil, then I saw the wheel go past me. I knew I was going to crash, I jumped on the brakes and tried to spin the car around. It's best to hit going backward, it distributes the shock more evenly over your body. Also, you can't see what you're going to hit! I took fifty miles an hour off it before I hit. I hung on, you'd better believe I hung on, until I felt the tail start to come up, I knew the car was going over, so I let go the wheel, I'd already bent it to a pretzel, I let myself go limp and I went out. Next thing I knew, I was on my hands and knees beside the road and I couldn't see and I couldn't breathe. And that frightened me. . . .

When I did the Portuguese [Grand Prix], a couple of months after the Spa crash, I remember feeling some fear. I was driving the same type of car I'd crashed at Spa, and that circuit is tree-lined and I remember going through a really fast corner, 130 miles an hour or something like that and the idea flashed through my mind, what would happen if a wheel came off *here?* All one can really do is put it out of one's mind. One's just got to conquer that. It isn't courage, it's just a case of overcoming whatever it is that worries you.

'MAN OVERBOARD'

In 1947, six brave men undertook an unusual voyage to test their theory that the ancient Indians of Peru could have sailed the 4,300 miles to Polynesia on rafts of balsa wood. On their primitive boat, the Kon-Tiki, *Norwegian captain Thor Heyerdahl and his five companions made their 101-day journey. Here Heyerdahl recalls one of their most terrifying experiences:*

We bellowed "Man overboard!" at the top of our lungs as we rushed to the nearest life-saving gear. The others had not heard Herman's cry because of the noise on deck. . . .

While Bengt and I launched the dinghy, Knut and Erick threw out the life belt. Carrying a long line, it hung ready for use on the corner of the cabin roof, but today the wind was so strong that when it was thrown it was simply blown back to the raft. After a few unsuccessful throws Herman was already far astern of the steering oar, swimming desperately to keep up with the raft, while the distance increased with each gust of wind. He realized that henceforth the gap would simply go on increasing, but he set a faint hope on the dinghy which we had now got into the water. Without the line, which acted as a brake, it would perhaps be possible to drive the rubber raft to meet the swimming man, but whether the rubber raft would ever get back to the *Kon-Tiki* was another matter. Nevertheless, three men in a rubber dinghy had some chance; one man in the sea had none.

Then we suddenly saw Knut take off and plunge head-first into the sea. He had the life belt in one hand and was heaving himself along. Every time Herman's head appeared on a wave back Knut was gone, and every time Knut came up Herman was not there. But then we saw both heads at once; they had swum to meet each other and both were hanging on to the life belt. Knut waved his arm, and, as the rubber raft had meanwhile been hauled on board, all four of us took hold of the line of the life belt and hauled for dear life, with our eyes fixed on the great dark object which was visible just behind the two men. This same mysterious beast in the water was pushing a big greenish-black triangle up above the wave crests; it almost gave Knut a shock when he was on his way over to Herman. Only Herman knew then that the triangle did not belong to a shark or any other sea monster. It was an inflated corner of Torstein's watertight sleeping bag.

But the sleeping bag did not remain floating for long after we had hauled the two men safe and sound on board. Whatever dragged the sleeping bag down into the depths had just missed a better prey.

"Glad I wasn't in it," said Torstein and took hold of the steering oar where he had let it go.

But otherwise there were not many wisecracks that evening. We all felt a chill running through nerve and bone for a long time afterward. But the cold shivers were mingled with a warm thankfulness that there were still six of us on board.

We had a lot of nice things to say to Knut that day—Herman and the rest of us, too.

JOHN GLENN'S GLORY RIDE

Marine Colonel John Glenn was the first American astronaut to orbit the earth. During his space flight, on February 20, 1962, Colonel Glenn rode the Friendship 7 capsule with the cool grace of any literary hero. Journalist William Shelton writes of Glenn's harrowing return:

Unknown to John Glenn at the time, just as he entered his second orbit, one of the tracking stations received an ominous signal. If the signal were true, the big protective heat shield at the blunt end of the capsule had come ajar.

As ground station after ground station continued to receive a reading that the vital heat shield was loose, tension began to build up in Mercury Control. John Glenn wasn't told, at first, about the signal, but he soon began to suspect the difficulty from the urgent nature of the questions thrown at him from the ground.

Cape Canaveral was filled with experts on all aspects of the capsule, yet this problem was so unexpected and—at the same time—so urgent that outside consultants were called in.

The big question in all their minds was whether or not they should believe the indication that the switch which holds the heat shield on was actually open.

The only logical alternative that presented itself was to change the normal flight procedure and leave the retro package on during reentry.

The theory was that the three straps which held the retro package on would also—until they melted—hold the heat shield in place. After the straps melted, there should be sufficient atmospheric pressure to keep a loose shield in place. The only trouble with this procedure was that it had never been tested in anything except a wind tunnel. No one really knew if it would work in space. The decision not only involved a difficult "calculated risk," it also involved the survival of John Glenn. . . .

Word was flashed to Glenn from astronaut Wally

Schirra in Hawaii to leave the retros on. When the retros fired Glenn said, "It felt like I was going clear back to Hawaii." After retro firing, as he passed over the Corpus Christi tracking station, capsule communicator [called Texas cap com] George Guthrie asked him if he knew why he was told to leave the retros on. "Yes, I think I do," replied Glenn. But, as he went back to other duties, he gave no indication that he was unduly worried. The scene in Mercury Control, however, was one of hidden but deep and intensifying concern as the tracking boards showed Friendship 7 approaching the point of maximum pressure and heat. Even Shorty Powers, who tried to discipline himself to keep his voice calm, began to show the strain. As he announced that landing area weather was one-tenth cloud cover and ten miles visibility (very good) his voice had a worried edge. The concern was heightened by the fact that, as expected, all voice and radar contact with the spacecraft was lost during the most critical part of reentry. This was because the ionization layer that forms around the capsule during the searing heat of reentry blocks all radio signals.

After an agonizing period of over four minutes of radio silence, John Glenn's southern Ohio accent came on suddenly. "Boy," he said excitedly, "that was a real fireball." The world of Cape Canaveral and the world everywhere sighed in thankful relief. . . .

14

TO THE SUMMIT!

On June 2, 1953, Great Britain was to crown a new monarch, Elizabeth II. In the early morning hours, the news flashed that the summit of the highest mountain in the world had been conquered—and by a citizen of the British Commonwealth. Edmund Hillary of New Zealand had mastered Mount Everest. Five expeditions had preceded his. Each had failed, all with loss of life. In his book High Adventure, *Sir Edmund Hillary recalls those last few steps he took to the summit:*

I lay on the little rock ledge panting furiously. Gradually it dawned on me that I was up the step and I felt a glow of pride and determination that completely subdued my temporary feelings of weakness. For the first time on the whole expedition I knew I was going to get to the top. "It will have to be pretty tough to stop us now" was my thought. But I couldn't entirely ignore the feeling of astonishment and wonder that I'd been able to get up such a difficulty at 29,000 feet even with oxygen. . . .

We were getting desperately tired now and Tenzing was going very slowly. I'd been cutting steps for almost two hours and my back and arms were starting to tire. I tried cramponing along the slope without cutting steps, but my feet slipped uncomfortably down the slope. I went on cutting. We seemed to have

We were on the summit of Everest. It was 11:30 A.M. My first sensation was one of relief-- relief that the long grind was over....

been going for a very long time and my confidence was fast evaporating. Bump followed bump with maddening regularity. A patch of shingle barred our way and I climbed dully up it and started cutting steps around another bump. And then I realized that this was the last bump, for ahead of me the ridge dropped steeply away in a great corniced curve, and out in the distance I could see the pastel shades and fleecy clouds of the highlands of Tibet. . . .

Peering from side to side and thrusting with my ice ax I tried to discover a possible cornice, but everything seemed solid and firm. I waved Tenzing up to me. A few more whacks of the ice ax, a few very weary steps and we were on the summit of Everest.

It was 11:30 A.M. My first sensation was one of relief—relief that the long grind was over; that the summit had been reached before our oxygen supplies had dropped to a critical level; and relief that in the end the mountain had been kind to us in having a pleasantly rounded cone for its summit instead of a fearsome and unapproachable cornice. But mixed with the relief was a vague sense of astonishment that I should have been the lucky one to attain the ambition of so many brave and determined climbers. It seemed difficult at first to grasp that we'd got there. I was too tired and too conscious of the long way down to safety really to feel any great elation. But as the fact of our success thrust itself more clearly into my mind I felt a quiet glow of satisfaction spread through my body—a satisfaction less vociferous but more powerful than I had ever felt on a mountaintop before.

THE LAST MARCH

Robert Falcon Scott was a Captain in the British Navy whose dream was to be the first man to reach the South Pole. In 1911 Scott and his expedition made the tortuous trip across the Antarctic—only to discover that the Norwegian, Amundsen, had beaten them to the Pole by a few weeks. The following passages are from Scott's journal, which describes the ill-fated return journey:

Wednesday, February 22.—R. 36. Supper Temp. $-2°$. There is little doubt we are in for a rotten critical time going home, and the lateness of the season may make it really serious. . . .

Friday, March 2.—Lunch. Misfortunes rarely come singly. We marched to the [Middle Barrier] depot fairly easily yesterday afternoon, and since that have suffered three distinct blows which have placed us in a bad position. First we found a shortage of oil; with most rigid economy it can scarce carry us to the next depot on this surface [71 miles away]. Second, Titus Oates disclosed his feet, the toes showing very bad indeed, evidently bitten by the late temperatures. The third blow came in the night, when the wind, which we had hailed with some joy, brought dark overcast weather. It fell below 40° in the night, and this morning it took 1½ hours to get our foot gear on, but we got away before eight. We lost cairn [stones set up as landmarks for the return trip] and tracks together and made as steady as we could N. by W., but have seen nothing. . . .

Monday, March 5.—Lunch. Regret to say going from bad to worse. . . . Marched for 5 hours this morning over slightly better surface covered with high moundy sastrugi. Sledge capsized twice; we pulled on foot, covering about 5½ miles. We are two pony marches and 4 miles about from our depot. Our fuel dreadfully low and the poor Soldier [Oates] nearly done. It is pathetic enough because we can do nothing for him; more hot food might do a little, but only a little, I fear. We none of us expected these terribly low temperatures, and of the rest of us Wilson is feeling them most; mainly, I fear, from his self-sacrificing devotion in doctoring Oates' feet.

Saturday, March 10.—Things steadily downhill. Oates' foot worse. He has rare pluck and must know that he can never get through. He asked Wilson if he had a chance this morning, and of course Bill had to say he didn't know. In point of fact he has none. Apart from him, if he went under now, I doubt whether we could get through. With great care we might have a dog's chance, but no more. The weather conditions are awful, and our gear gets steadily more icy and difficult to manage. . . .

Friday, March 16 or Saturday 17.—Lost track of dates, but think the last correct. Tragedy all along the line. At lunch, the day before yesterday, poor Titus Oates said he couldn't go on; he proposed we should leave him in his sleeping-bag. That we could not do, and we induced him to come on, on the afternoon march. In spite of its awful nature for him he struggled on and we made a few miles. At night he was worse and we knew the end had come.

Should this be found I want these facts recorded. Oates' last thoughts were of his Mother, but immediately before he took pride in thinking that his regiment would be pleased with the bold way in which he met his death. We can testify to his bravery. He has borne intense suffering for weeks without complaint, and to the very last was able and willing to discuss outside subjects. He did not—would not—give up hope til the very end. He was a brave soul. This was the end. He slept through the night before last, hoping not to wake; but he woke in the morning—yesterday. It was blowing a blizzard. He said, "I am just going outside and may be some time." He went out into the blizzard and we have not seen him since.

Thursday, March 29.—Since the 21st we have had a

There is little doubt we are in for a rotten critical time going home, and the lateness of the season may make it really serious.

continuous gale from W.S.W. and S.W. We had fuel to make two cups of tea apiece and bare food for two days on the 20th. Every day we have been ready to start for our depot 11 *miles* away, but outside the door of the tent it remains a scene of whirling drift. I do not think we can hope for any better things now. We shall stick it out to the end. But we are getting weaker, of course, and the end cannot be far.

It seems a pity, but I do not think I can write more.

R. Scott

Last entry.—For God's sake look after our people.

The entire party perished. The journal was later found beside Scott's body.

'SHAKE HANDS WITH A LION'

Helen Keller, though blind and deaf, wrote fluently, eloquently, and with deep understanding. Her books reveal her personal courage as does this unusual and dramatic episode in her life:

When Helen Keller, in front of the lion cage at the zoo, said she was going inside to get better acquainted, she was told it was absolutely impossible. The particular lion in there was tough, from Africa. She gave reasons. She had been studying all she could about lions and was sure she could manage. Somehow she got her way.

The lion was surprised. He had never seen a human being like this one. Of course he couldn't understand that here was a famous woman who was not only blind. She was deaf as well. But he could sense perhaps that she had the gift of empathy, of identifying herself with other creatures. Anyway, as she stretched out her hands inquiringly and started walking directly toward him, he offered no resistance.

In front of him she kneeled with a sort of contagious reverence for the way he was put together. Down his back she ran her sensitive fingers. Yes, the mane was just as the books had described it and so was the fur on the tail. But what's this, at the very end? This tuft of long hairs! Nobody had mentioned that. How interesting. How funny.

The exploring touch went down one leg to the paw. The lion cooperatively lifted it. She felt the claws, one after the other, then the pad, up and down.

Here, that's enough! said the lion. And he made a great noise. But Helen Keller didn't hear though the vibrations must have startled her. Showing no shock or anxiety, she continued testing out each paw and leg muscle.

Satisfied, she stood up and lifted her hands in a gesture of wonder and admiration. Taking her time she found her way to the door of the cage and rejoined her friends who were once more breathing freely.

'AN INDESTRUCTIBLE RADIANCE'

In his book Party of One, *Clifton Fadiman describes with reverence the lives of Marie and Pierre Curie, the discoverers of radium. Throughout her life, Marie Curie fought seemingly unsurmountable obstacles with perseverance and endurance. In this section, Clifton Fadiman describes her unwavering devotion to science:*

It is hard to think of many first-rate scientific careers in which some major flaw of character does not show itself, confounding our natural desire for wholehearted hero worship. But the lives of Marie and Pierre Curie, two of the most beautiful lives, I suppose, that have ever been lived, provided an exception. It was almost theatrically apt that this man and woman, with characters of shining purity, should have built their careers around a physical element recognized by its indestructible and essential radiance. . . .

"She did not know how to be famous," says Eve Curie in her classic biography of her mother. In one deliberate sentence she strikes to the heart of the secret: "I hope that the reader may constantly feel, across the ephemeral movement of one existence, what in Marie Curie was even more rare than her work or her life: the immovable structure of a character; the stubborn effort of an intelligence; the free immolation of a human being that could give all and take nothing, could even receive nothing; and above all the quality of a soul in which neither fame nor adversity could change the exceptional purity.". . .

The childhood is unhappy, torn by the death of mother and eldest sister, rendered overserious by poverty, given a certain tenseness by the fact that she is a member of a subject race, the Poles. . . . The little child who at five stood in rapt awe before her father's case containing the "phys-ics ap-pa-ra-tus" reawakens in the girl of eighteen. Her duties as a governess do not prevent her from studying. She has no money, not even for stamps so that she may write to her brother. But "I am learning chemistry from a book.". . .

On forty rubles a month [Marie] Sklodowska lives, studies, learns. Solitude, near-starvation, an unheated garret—none of these things matters, as long as at least a part of her day is spent in the laboratory. . . .

In 1894 she meets Pierre Curie, already a physicist of note, a mind "both powerful and noble.". . . It is a perfect marriage, the marriage not merely of two people who love each other but, what is incomparably more interesting and important, of two great physicists who can help each other. It is Marie, attracted by the uranium researches of Becquerel, who starts herself and her husband on the long, tedious, glorious path at the end of which lies radium. They know that radium and polonium . . . exist, but they must prove it. From 1898 to 1902, in a dilapidated, leaking, freezing shed, with primitive apparatus, with little or no help, unaided by the scientific bureaucracy or by the State, these two gentle fanatics work in an absorption that is like a dream. . . . With "her terrible patience," Marie, doing the work of four strong men, pounds away at her chemical masses, boils, separates, refines, stirs, strains. Somewhere in this inert brown stuff lies radium. Marie loses fifteen pounds during these five years. At last they isolate the element.

All this time they have been bringing up a family. They have had sorrows, family illnesses. Pierre's mother has died of the very disease against which radium is soon to prove a weapon. . . .

In 1903 the Curies, with Becquerel, receive the Nobel Prize for Physics. The world pursues them. Now they must flee the world. "In science we must be interested in things, not persons," says Marie, who was never to be interested in herself. . . .

Then on April 19, 1906, Aeschylean tragedy, cutting Marie's life in two, giving it at the same time a new emotional dimension. Pierre's head is crushed by a van in a street accident, and Marie becomes "a pitiful and incurably lonely woman." She refuses a pension (always the State makes its generous offers too late); she proceeds with the education of her daughters; she takes over Pierre's teaching post and, in a dry, monotonous voice, without making any reference to her predecessor, resumes the lectures at the exact point at which Pierre had left off.

The rest of her life is the story of her marriage with radium. . . . Almost blind, her hands and arms scarred, pitted, and burned by thirty years of radium emanations, she continues her work almost to the day of her death, caused in part by that very element which she had released for the use of mankind.

'THE SPIRIT OF ST. LOUIS'

Charles Lindbergh was the first man to fly non-stop and alone between America and Europe. His 1927 flight accelerated international interest in aviation and captured the imaginations of millions. In this selection from his book The Spirit of St. Louis, *"Lucky Lindy" describes one of many dangerous encounters:*

It's cold up here at—I glance at the altimeter—10,500 feet—*cold*—good Lord, there *are* things to be considered outside the cockpit! How could I forget! I jerk off a leather mitten and thrust my arm out the window. My palm is covered with stinging pinpricks. I pull the flashlight from my pocket and throw its beam onto a strut. The entering edge is irregular and shiny—*ice!* And as far out into darkness as the

*Can those be
   the same stars?
Is this the same sky?
How bright! How clear!
What safety I have
      reached!*

Spirit of St. Louis

beam penetrates, the night is filled with countless, horizontal, threadlike streaks. The venturi tubes may clog at any moment!

I've got to turn around, get back into clear air—quickly! . . .

I keep pressing rudder cautiously until the turn indicator's needle creeps a quarter-inch to the left. . . .

"Turn faster! You see the air speed's dropping. It's ice doing that! Quick, or it'll be too late!"

"No, it's not ice—at least not likely. It's probably just the normal slowing down in a bank."

"But the altimeter's dropping too! It's ice, I tell you."

I open the throttle another 50 revolutions. I don't dare push the stick forward very much to gain speed. The *Spirit of St. Louis* is too close to the top of the main cloud layer. There were less than a thousand feet to spare when I entered the thunderhead. That endless stratus layer is probably full of ice too. If I drop down into it, I may never see the stars again. . . .

I ought to be turned around now—Center the turn indicator—level out the plane—flashlight onto the liquid compass. . . .

I bank again and glance at the altimeter—10,300 feet. Good—it's gone up a little. I throw my flashlight onto the wing strut. Ice is thicker!

The earth-inductor needle begins moving backward, jumping erratically—Level out wings—About the right heading this time. Now, if the turn indicator doesn't ice up for a few minutes more—I put my hand out the window again—the pinpricks are still there.

Steady the plane. Make the compass card stop swinging—but the air's too rough—Is the turn-indicator getting sluggish—icing?—It seems to move back and forth more slowly—Everything depends on its working till I get outside this cloud—Just two or three more minutes—

My eyes sense a change in the blackness of my cockpit. I look out through the window. Can those be the same stars? Is this the same sky? How bright! How clear! What safety I have reached! Bright, clear, safe? But this is the same air I left, the same fraction of an earthly hour. I've simply been existing in a different frame of space and time. Values are relative, dependent on one's circumstance. They change from frame to frame, and as one travels back and forth between them. Here I've found security where I left danger, flying over a major storm, above a frigid northern ocean. Here's something I never saw before—the brilliant light of a black night.

The Courage of Conviction

KEEPING IDEALS

Despite the horrors of Nazism that kept the Otto Frank family hiding in a few rooms for two years, the Frank's teen-age daughter, Anne, did not dwell on their miseries, but on the 'beauty that still remains':

It's really a wonder that I haven't dropped all my ideals, because they seem so absurd and impossible to carry out. Yet I keep them, because in spite of everything I still believe that people are really good at heart. I simply can't build my hopes on a foundation consisting of confusion, misery, and death. I see the world gradually being turned into a wilderness, I hear the ever approaching thunder, which will destroy us too, I can feel the sufferings of millions and yet, if I look up into the heavens, I think that it will all come right, that this cruelty too will end, and that peace and tranquility will return again. In the meantime, I must uphold my ideals, for perhaps the time will come when I shall be able to carry them out.

A few days after this diary entry, the Nazis raided the Franks' hideout and they were deported and interned in concentration camps. Anne's father alone survived.

And yet to me it's one of the perpetual astonishments of a war life that human beings recover as quickly as they do.

'THE HUMAN SPIRIT IS LIKE A CORK'

Ernie Pyle was one of the greatest war correspondents of all time. His highly personal accounts of men under fire, in all branches of the military, brought home the grim realities of World War II—but not without a lighter side, too, for Ernie Pyle also conveyed the soldier's ability to keep his cool, his wit, his laughter in the face of danger. The following selection is from Brave Men, *which contains stories of the war in Europe during 1943-44:*

The awarding of bravery medals is a rather dry and formal thing and I had never bothered to cover any such festivities. One night, however, I learned that three old friends of mine were in a group to be decorated, so I went down to have supper with them and see the show. . . .

After supper the six men and three officers who were to receive awards lined up outside the tent. They were nine legitimate heroes all right, I know, for I was in the vicinity when they did their deed:

It was the night before my birthday and the German bombers kept us awake all night with their flares and their bombings, and for a while it looked as though I might never get to be forty-three years old. What happened in this special case was that one of our generator motors caught fire during the night and it had to happen at a very inopportune moment.

When the next wave of bombers came over, the Germans naturally used the fire as a target.

The three officers and six MPs dashed to the fire to put it out. They stuck right at their work as the Germans dived on them. They stayed while the bombs blasted around them and shrapnel flew. I was sleeping about a quarter of a mile away, and the last stick of bombs almost seemed to blow me out of the bedroll—so you can visualize what those men went through. The nine of them were awarded the Silver Star. . . .

A soldier who has been a long time in the line does have a "look" in his eyes that anyone who knows about it can discern. It's a look of dullness, eyes that look without seeing, eyes that see without conveying any image to the mind. It's a look that is the display room for what lay behind it—exhaustion, lack of sleep, tension for too long, weariness that is too great, fear beyond fear, misery to the point of numbness, a look of surpassing indifference to anything anybody can do. It's a look I dread to see on men.

And yet to me it's one of the perpetual astonishments of a war life that human beings recover as quickly as they do. For example, a unit may be pretty well exhausted, but if they are lucky enough to be blessed with some sunshine and warmth they'll begin to be normal after two days out of the line. The human spirit is just like a cork. . . .

34

'A LOGIC OF COURAGE'

Author and world traveler Lowell Thomas contrasts life of the nuclear age with a story of personal bravery in the 18th century:

In these atomic times, when so many people are trembling about the "ultimate disaster," I find that there is a sort of steadying strength in the following story:

It was on May 19, 1780—during the anxious days of our Revolutionary War—that darkness came at noon. The bats flew and chickens roosted. It was some sort of meteorological phenomenon that seemed to bring the day to an end when the sun was at zenith. Panic broke out, and people thought that the end of the world was at hand.

At Hartford, Connecticut, the State Legislature was in session and, when the darkness came at noon, the meeting of the Lower House broke up in alarm. In the State Senate a motion of adjournment was made, so that the legislators could meet the Day of Judgment with whatever courage they could manage to summon.

But the motion was opposed by Abraham Davenport, a Yankee selectman and judge, friend and adviser of George Washington. Abraham Davenport faced the panic about the end of the world with the best of Yankee heart and head.

He arose and addressed his legislative colleagues.

"I am against this adjournment," he said. Then he explained with a logic of courage:

"The Day of Judgment," he said, "is either approaching or it is not. If it is not, there is no cause for adjournment. If it is, I choose to be found doing my duty. I wish, therefore, that candles may be brought."

Of course, this was not the only time that people have beheld what seems to be the ultimate disaster. In the past they have trembled in the presence of such nightmares as the invasion of the Huns led by Attila, the Scourge of God, or the rage of plagues like the Black Death, or the predicted end of the world in the year 1000.

But in all history it would be hard to find a better example for our times than the sturdy figure of Abraham Davenport. At a time when we are all haunted by doubts and questions about the possibility of atomic war and trying to decide what course to take, he gives us the only possible answer: "I choose to be found doing my duty."

'A CLARION CALL SOUNDED'

Eleanor Roosevelt's long-time friend Fannie Hurst, author of many bestselling novels, including Back Street *and* Imitation of Life, *wrote a short portrait of Mrs. Roosevelt that stands out as a sympathetic and intimate study of a woman known for her devotion to public service. Here, Miss Hurst describes her friend Eleanor Roosevelt*:

Every nook and corner of the Eleanor Roosevelt personality has been explored and evaluated, except perhaps the tiny mosaics of her every-day humanness that shine like tiny chip-diamonds through her grandeur.

Be that as it may, only time, which creates its classics, will determine the ultimate evaluation. Mine, however, persists. Eleanor Roosevelt was one of the first, if not the first, ladies of the world, the list exotic and highly limited.

Yet this great lady was something of a paradox. She was not an intellectual; she belonged to no high-level establishment, but far beyond, she operated through intelligence, her humanness and humanity infallible. . . .

Eleanor Roosevelt grew into her greatness. After an orphaned but carefully nurtured girlhood, well schooled privately in the United States and France, the girl who married her cousin, the highly eligible Franklin Delano Roosevelt, man of destiny, did not presage the ultimate woman who was to emerge from the baptism-of-fire years that followed.

First, of course, were the child-bearing years, always under the domination of an overpowering mother-in-law, who had never cut the umbilical cord that bound her son to her and who was to spread darkly the immensity of her maternal wings over the young wifehood of her daughter-in-law.

The emergence of Eleanor Roosevelt from her imprisonment in those early years dates from the shattering circumstance of Franklin Roosevelt's poliomyelitis. It was subsequent to this calamity that a clarion call sounded with Eleanor, and, almost instantly, she became legs and messenger for a husband who was to remain almost chairbound for the historically meaningful years of his life.

The nation reacted variously to this emergence from housewife into world activities, mostly critically. What is the big idea, the first lady of the land gallivanting over the country? Woman's place is in the home, commandingly so when that home happens to be the White House. . . .

She was not only aware of the immensity of her problems as a kind of conveyer-belt to her husband but also, in the midst of climax after climax, was able to laugh over the foibles of the world swirling so rapidly around her.

I recall one day, lunching at the White House with members of the family, my amazement when the First Lady walked into the dining room clad in pants and sweater. "My mother-in-law detests these togs and I couldn't resist," she whispered to me, humanness out all over her. . . .

Certainly the "humanness" alone of Eleanor Roosevelt does not add up to the ultimate grandeur of this woman through the years that were to call forth qualities that must have been inherent but might have gone unrealized. The Eleanor Roosevelt of a rather undistinguished girlhood and a wifehood which began under the domination of her mother-in-law scarcely presaged the opening of the folded wings within the heart and soul of this woman. Destiny leaned into her life and she took flight into world realms.

'I'VE BEEN TO THE MOUNTAIN TOP'

The day before Martin Luther King, Jr., was assassinated, he expressed his faith in the "promised land," although he saw "difficult days ahead":
Well, I don't know what will happen now. We've got some difficult days ahead. But it really doesn't matter with me now. Because I've been to the mountain top. I won't mind.

Like anybody, I would like to live a long life. Longevity has its place. But I'm not concerned about that now. I just want to do God's will.

And He's allowed me to go up to the mountain. And I've looked over, and I've seen the promised land.

I've got to keep on until I can quit honorably. All I'm fighting for now is my own self-respect.

I may not get there with you, but I want you to know tonight that we as a people will get to the promised land.

So I'm happy tonight. I'm not fearing any man. Mine eyes have seen the glory of the coming of the Lord.

FIGHTING FOR SELF-RESPECT

A special brand of bravery must be accorded the daredevil flyers of World War I—men often considered more crazy than courageous. The following selection is taken from the diary of an unknown aviator, who was later shot down and killed in aerial combat:

I'm sick. At night when the colonel calls up to give us our orders, my ears are afire until I hear what we are to do the next morning. Then I can't sleep for thinking about it all night. And while I'm waiting around all day for the afternoon patrol, I think I am going crazy. I keep watching the clock and figuring how long I have to live. Then I go out to test out my engine and guns and walk around and have a drink and try to write a little and try not to think. And I move my arms and legs around and think that perhaps to-morrow I won't be able to. . . .

It gives me a dizzy feeling every time I hear of the men that are gone. And they have gone so fast I can't keep track of them; every time two pilots meet it is only to swap news of who's killed. When a person takes sick, lingers in bed a few days, dies, and is buried on the third day, it all seems regular and they pass on into the great beyond in an orderly manner and you accept their departure as an accomplished fact. But when you lunch with a man, talk to him, see him go out and get in his plane in the prime of his youth and the next day someone tells you that he is dead—it just doesn't sink in and you can't believe it. And the oftener it happens the harder it is to believe. I've lost over a hundred friends, so they tell me,— I've seen only seven or eight killed—but to me they aren't dead yet. They are just around the corner, I think, and I'm still expecting to run into them any time. I dream about them at night when I do sleep a little and sometimes I dream that some one is killed who really isn't. Then I don't know who is and who isn't. . . .

I only hope I can stick it out and not turn yellow. I've heard of men landing in Germany when they didn't have to. They'd be better off dead because they've got to live with themselves the rest of their lives. I wouldn't mind being shot down; I've got no taste for glory and I'm no more good, but I've got to keep on until I can quit honorably. All I'm fighting for now is my own self-respect.

Heroism in War

THE LADY WITH A LAMP

With wealthy parents, personal beauty, and accomplished wit, Florence Nightingale was destined to become a sheltered British socialite. She became instead a nurse and left England for the Barrack Hospital in the Crimea to tend thousands of wounded British soldiers under deplorable conditions. Here her biographer, Cecil Woodham-Smith, describes her welcome:
On November 5 [1854] Miss Nightingale and her party were welcomed into the Barrack Hospital with every attention and escorted into the hospital with compliments and expressions of goodwill. When they saw their quarters, the picture abruptly changed. . . .

Fourteen nurses were to sleep in one room, ten nuns in another; Miss Nightingale and Mrs. Bracebridge shared the closet. . . . There was no furniture, no food, no means of cooking food, no beds.

As the fierce winter set in and the Russian Armies inflicted heavy losses on the English forces, the situation became critical for the wounded: In January, 1855, there were 12,000 men in hospital and only 11,000 in the camp before Sebastopol; and still the shiploads came pouring down. It was, Miss Nightingale wrote, "calamity unparalleled in the history of calamity."

In this emergency she became supreme. She was the rock to which everyone clung. . . .

Her calmness, her resource, her power to take action raised her to the position of a goddess. The men adored her. "If she were at our head," they said, "we should be in Sebastopol next week." The doctors came to be absolutely dependent on her. . . .

Sidney Herbert [Secretary of War] had asked her to write to him privately in addition to her official reports, and during her time in Scutari and the Crimea she wrote him a series of over thirty letters of enormous length, crammed with detailed and practical suggestions for the reform of the present system. It is almost incredible that in addition to the unceasing labor she was performing, when she was living in the foul atmosphere of the Barrack Hospital incessantly harried by disputes, callers, complaints and overwhelmed with official correspondence which had to be written in her own hand, she should have found time and energy to write this long series of vast, carefully thought-out letters, many as long as a pamphlet. She never lost sight of the main issue. . . . She wrote: "There is a far greater question to be agitated before the country than that of these eighty-four miserable women—eighty-five including me. This is whether the system or no system which is found adequate in

When a flood
of sick came in,
she was on her feet
for twenty-four hours
at a stretch....

time of peace but wholly inadequate to meet the exigencies of a time of war is to be left as it is—*or* patched up temporarily, as you give a beggar half pence—or made equal to the wants not diminishing but increasing in a time of awful pressure...."

She asked nothing for herself, nor did she use her influence to make life easier for herself by securing advancement for her friends....

Her facts and figures were freely used by Sidney Herbert and other members of the Cabinet, and important changes made in British Army organization during the course of the Crimean War were based on her suggestions. A Medical School was founded during the campaign, and the suggestions respecting the Purveyor, though not carried out immediately, formed the basis of reforms executed at a later date....

When a flood of sick came in, she was on her feet for twenty-four hours at a stretch. She was known to pass eight hours on her knees dressing wounds.... It was her rule never to let any man who came under her observation die alone. If he were conscious, she herself stayed beside him; if he were unconscious she sometimes allowed Mrs. Bracebridge to take her place. She estimated that during that winter she witnessed 2,000 deathbeds. The worst cases she nursed herself.... One of the nurses described accompanying her on her night rounds. "It seemed an endless walk. . . . As we slowly passed along the silence was profound; very seldom did a moan or cry from those deeply suffering fall on our ears. A dim light burned here and there. Miss Nightingale carried her lantern which she would set down before she bent over any of the patients. I much admired her manner to the men—it was so tender and kind."

'WHY FRANCO NEVER TOOK MADRID'

From 1937 to 1939, American journalist and author Ernest Hemingway reported for newspapers on the events in the Spanish Civil War. Of the Spaniards he writes, "They are tough and they are efficient." Here Hemingway describes his driver Hipolito, who inspired this evaluation:

Hipolito was not much taller than Tomás [the previous chauffeur], but he looked carved out of a granite block. He walked with a roll, putting his feet down flat at each stride; and he had an automatic pistol so big it came halfway down his leg. He always said "Salud" with a rising inflection as though it were something you said to hounds. Good hounds that knew their business. He knew motors, he could drive and if you told him to show up at six a.m., he was there ten minutes before the hour. . . .

He was our chauffeur in Madrid and at the front

during a nineteen-day bombardment of the capital that was almost too bad to write anything about. All the time he was as solid as the rock he looked to be cut from, as sound as a good bell and as regular and accurate as a railway man's watch. He made you realize why Franco never took Madrid when he had the chance.

Hipolito and the others like him would have fought from street to street, and house to house, as long as any one of them was left alive; and the last ones left would have burned the town. They are tough and they are efficient. They are the Spaniards that once conquered the Western World. They are not romantic like the Anarchists and they are not afraid to die. Only they never mention it. . . .

The details of that day are a little confused because after nineteen days of heavy shelling some of the days get merged into others; but at one o'clock the shelling stopped and we decided to go to the Hotel Gran Via, about six blocks down, to get some lunch. I was going to walk by a very tortuous and extremely safe way I had worked out utilizing the angles of least danger, when Hipolito said, "Where are you going?"

"To eat."

"Get in the car."

"You're crazy."

"Come on, we'll drive down the Gran Via. It's stopped. They are eating their lunch too."

Four of us got into the car and drove down the Gran Via. It was solid with broken glass. There were great holes all down the sidewalks. Buildings were smashed and we had to walk around a heap of rubble and a smashed stone cornice to get into the hotel. There was not a living person on either side of the street, which had been, always, Madrid's Fifth Avenue and Broadway combined. There were many dead. We were the only motor car.

Hipolito put the car up a side street and we all ate together. We were still eating when Hipolito finished and went up to the car. There was some more shelling sounding, in the hotel basement, like muffled blasting, and when we finished the lunch of bean soup, paper thin sliced sausage and an orange, we went upstairs, the streets were full of smoke and clouds of dust. There was new smashed cement work all over the sidewalk. I looked around a corner for the car. There was rubble scattered all down the street from a new shell that had hit just overhead. I saw the car. It was covered with dust and rubble.

"My God," I said, "they've got Hipolito."

He was lying with his head back in the driver's seat. I went to him feeling very badly. I had got very fond of Hipolito.

Hipolito was asleep.

"I thought you were dead," I said. He woke and wiped a yawn on the back of his hand.

"Que va, hombre," he said. "I am always accustomed to sleep after lunch if I have time."

"We are going to Chicote's Bar," I said.

"Have they got good coffee there?"

"Excellent."

"Come on," he said. "Let's go."

I tried to give him some money when I left Madrid.

"I don't want anything from you," he said.

"No," I said. "Take it. Go on. Buy something for the family."

"No," he said. "Listen, we had a good time, didn't we?"

You can bet on Franco, or Mussolini, or Hitler, if you want. But my money goes on Hipolito.

HE JARRED THE SAGGING CHINS

On November 12, 1942, U.S. Air Corps Captain Eddie Rickenbacker and the six surviving members of his crew were rescued from their life rafts in the Pacific Ocean—after 21 days at sea. In his book Seven Came Through, *Captain Rickenbacker describes the horrors of the ordeal and the faith and courage that sustained him and his men:*

Either the fourteenth night, or the night before, an unexpected and depressing event occurred. After

Alex died, I began to despair of Adamson. The nagging pain in his back, aggravated by salt-water sores, gave him no peace. To my knowledge he never slept deeply. He just slipped off into a permanent semi-consciousness, occasionally broken by feeble gusts of fury and intolerable pain. His feet, legs, arms, wrists, and face had been burned to a red pulp and any movement in the raft, however slight, was certain to communicate itself to his back.

Hans Adamson is an old and dear friend. It was a terrible responsibility to sit there and watch the strength go out of him. His clothes were rotting on his back. The colonel's eagles on his tunic were corroded. His uniform shirt and pants were water-stained and coming to pieces. A gray stubble covered his face, and his eyes were bloodshot and swollen.

On this particular night I felt the raft give a violent lurch. My first thought was that a shark was attacking. Adamson's body was no longer against mine. His end of the raft was empty. I saw something struggling in the water close by and my hand gripped Adamson's shoulder. He was too heavy for me to hold up alone, but my yells for help brought Cherry and Whittaker up in their raft. We were a long time at it, but we managed to haul him back into the raft.

In the morning Hans had a long, lucid interval. We talked about many things, familiar and pleasant things done together, the mission we were on. But from that day on he seldom spoke or asked for anything.

It does us no dishonor to say that we were all becoming a little unhinged. We were unreasonable, at times, in our demands upon one another. Wrathful and profane words were exchanged over nothing at all. Every night the rafts were drawn together for prayer meeting. We continued to read from [crewman] Bartek's New Testament, now yellowed and stained by salt water. But one or two, who had been most fervent, became backsliders. Because their prayers were not answered within twenty-four or forty-eight hours, they condemned the Lord for His failure to save them. They wanted deliverance immediately.

I tried to impart my own philosophy to these men, hoping to stimulate their desire to carry on. It was based upon the simple observation that the longer I have had to suffer under trying circumstances, the more certain I was to appreciate my deliverance. This is part of the wisdom that comes to older men.

If that didn't work I would turn to the only other weapon left, and that was to brutalize and jar those whose chins sagged too far down on their chests. One man said to me across twenty feet of water [in another raft]: "Rickenbacker, you are the meanest, most cantankerous so-and-so that ever lived." Some of the things I said could have been a heavy weight on my conscience. But I felt better after we reached land. Several of the boys confessed that they once swore an oath to live for the sheer pleasure of burying me at sea.

There were occasions when I myself was pretty hard pressed: when my private store of aches and pains reduced me to something less than a good companion. My legs and hip were rather severely torn in the Atlanta crash. Right up to the time of the Pacific trip I was under regular diathermic and physiotherapeutic treatment. If anyone had told me I could live for twenty-one days with two other men in a space approximately nine feet by five, I would have said he was crazy. . . .

Naturally, as time went on, the days grew longer. We could see moving objects, we could see each other, we could see the waves breaking, the swells of the ocean. . . .

The nights grew more deadly. Some of the boys would talk in their sleep, others would cry out in nightmares, and at times I could hear some of them praying. Each period from darkness to daylight, seemed like eternity. Always I kept trying to think and rack my brain for a way out of our dilemma. I had never lost my belief that we would be found. How, where, or when, was what I was trying to think through. . . .

So hard did I think of the many possibilities that

during the last few nights, and particularly from midnight until dawn when the mist was at its worst, I would doze off and dream of having landed on an island where I found an old friend with a lovely home who was happy and glad to welcome us, and who put me up in a nice soft bed and gave me a most delicious breakfast, all I had to do was to wait until Mr. Stimson, Secretary of War, arrived at his office. . . .

Then as the gray dawn came over the horizon, I would awaken to find to my horror and amazement that I was still on the broad Pacific, with its thick mist and that everlasting rocking to and fro that goes with the ocean swells.

'THE MOSQUITO ARMADA'

Winston Churchill, Prime Minister of England during the Second World War, wrote afterward of the evacuation of the British Expeditionary Force from Dunkirk, a rescue unparalled in history:
It was plain that large numbers of [small] craft would be required for work on the beaches, in addition to bigger ships which could load in Dunkirk harbour. . . . At the same time lifeboats from liners in the London docks, tugs from the Thames, yachts, fishing craft, lighters, barges, and pleasure boats—anything that could be of use along the beaches—were called

into service. By the night of the 27th a great tide of small vessels began to flow towards the sea, first to our Channel ports, and thence to the beaches of Dunkirk and the beloved Army.

Once the need for secrecy was relaxed the Admiralty did not hesitate to give full rein to the spontaneous movement which swept the seafaring population of our south and southeastern shores. Everyone who had a boat of any kind, steam or sail, put out for Dunkirk, and the preparations, fortunately begun a week earlier, were now aided by the brilliant improvision of volunteers on an amazing scale. The numbers arriving on the 29th were small, but they were the forerunners of nearly four hundred small craft which from the 31st were destined to play a vital part in ferrying from the beaches to the off-lying ships almost a hundred thousand men. In these days I missed the head of my Admiralty map room, Captain Pim, and one or two other familiar faces. . . .

The enemy had closely followed the withdrawal, and hard fighting was incessant, especially on the flanks near Nieuport and Bergues [France]. As the evacuation went on the steady decrease in the number of troops, both British and French, was accompanied by a corresponding contraction of the defense. On the beaches, among the sand dunes, for three, four or five days scores of thousands of men dwelt under unrelenting air attack. Hitler's belief that the German

Air Force would render escape impossible, and that therefore he should keep his armoured formations for the final stroke of the campaign, was a mistaken but not unreasonable one.

Three factors falsified his expectations. First, the incessant air bombing of the masses of troops along the seashore did them very little harm. The bombs plunged into the soft sand, which muffled their explosions. In the early stages, after a crashing air raid, the troops were astonished to find that hardly anybody had been killed or wounded. Everywhere there had been explosions, but scarcely anyone was the worse. A rocky shore would have produced far more deadly results. Presently the soldiers regarded the air attacks with contempt. They crouched in the sand dunes with composure and growing hope. Before them lay the grey but not unfriendly sea. Beyond, the rescuing ships and—Home.

The second factor which Hitler had not foreseen was the slaughter of his airmen. British and German air quality was put directly to the test. By intense effort Fighter Command maintained successive patrols over the scene, and fought the enemy at long odds. Hour after hour they bit into the German fighter and bomber squadrons, taking a heavy toll, scattering them and driving them away. Day after day this went on, till the glorious victory of the Royal Air Force was gained. Wherever German aircraft

In the midst of our defeat glory came to the island people, united and unconquerable....

were encountered, sometimes in forties and fifties, they were instantly attacked, often by single squadrons or less, and shot down in scores, which presently added up into hundreds. . . .

But all the aid of the sand and all the prowess in the air would have been vain without the sea. The instructions given ten or twelve days before had, under the pressure and emotion of events, borne amazing fruit. Perfect discipline prevailed ashore and afloat. The sea was calm. To and fro between the shore and the ships plied the little boats, gathering the men from the beaches as they waded out or picking them from the water, with total indifference to the air bombardment, which often claimed its victims. Their numbers alone defied air attack. The Mosquito Armada as a whole was unsinkable. In the midst of our defeat glory came to the island people, united and unconquerable; and the tale of the Dunkirk beaches will shine in whatever records are preserved of our affairs. . . .

JFK'S PT-109

In 1943, the late John F. Kennedy was a Lieutenant, J.G., in the United States Navy, serving as commander of a PT boat in the South Pacific. Around two in the morning of August 2, Kennedy's boat was rammed and split in two by the Japanese destroyer Amagiri. *Kennedy's courage and leadership during the next six days kept his crewmen alive and led to their eventual rescue. The following selections are from the book* PT-109 *by Robert J. Donovan*:

As the fire on the water around the boat subsided, Kennedy concluded that there would be no explosion. He and Maguire and Mauer swam back to the bow of the boat and climbed up on the deck. At Kennedy's direction Mauer got out the blinker, a two-foot-long tube with a light inside, and started walking around the hulk, flashing the light periodically as a beacon to any members of the crew who might still be alive.

Kennedy removed his shoes, shirt and sidearms and dived overboard in a rubber lifebelt to search for the others. He was to be in the water approximately thirty of the next thirty-six hours....

Periodically, Kennedy would pause and call "Where are you?" and Harris would answer "Over here." Harris heard the splashing grow louder, and then he saw Kennedy's head coming out of the dark. McMahon lay helpless in his kapok. Despite the cooling effect of the water his whole body felt warm.

"McMahon is too hurt to swim," Harris told Kennedy.

"All right, I'll take him back," Kennedy said. "Part of the boat is still floating."

Kennedy did not mention any other names, but the

sound of voices in the distance lifted Harris' spirits. McMahon, however, was without hope. He could not use his arms at all.

"Go on, skipper," the crew's "old man" mumbled to Kennedy. "You go on. I've had it."

Kennedy clutched McMahon's kapok and began towing him toward the boat, which by this time had drifted a considerable distance from the swimmers. The men aboard kept calling to give their position, and Kennedy followed the sound. At first Harris stayed abreast of Kennedy and McMahon despite his numb leg. Then, his strength on the wane, he dropped behind. "Come on," Kennedy urged him. Harris resumed swimming, but the burden seemed unendurable. His left leg dragged. He was drowsy. It felt luxurious just to slump back in his kapok and drift. Drawing farther and farther away, Kennedy would call back to him, and he would respond by lifting his heavy arms to swim awhile. Then, tiring, he would drift again. . . .

It seemed as though he was alone for a half-hour or longer before he again heard Kennedy splashing toward him, calling, "Where are you, Harris?" As Kennedy reappeared, Harris wearily told him, "I can't go any further."

"For a guy from Boston, you're certainly putting up a great exhibition out here, Harris," Kennedy snapped.

Harris cursed and swore at Kennedy. He was aggrieved that Kennedy did not realize how much his leg troubled him. "Well, come on," Kennedy persisted. Harris asked the skipper to hold him up while he took off his kapok to shed his sweater and jacket. Kennedy gripped his arm and held him precariously on the surface. Had the exhausted and dispirited Harris slipped from Kennedy's grasp he might have gone down like a stone. But with his heavy clothes and his shoes off and his kapok back on, Harris found he could move through the water, and he and Kennedy swam slowly back to the boat.

Set in Linotype Times Roman, designed by
Stanley Morison in 1931 for The London Times.
Typography by Grant Dahlstrom,
and set at The Castle Press.
Printed on Hallmark Eggshell Book paper.
Designed by William M. Gilmore.